BOOK OF
REVELATION

MADE EASY

D1713267

ROSE
PUBLISHING

Published by Rose Publishing
An imprint of Tyndale House Ministries
Carol Stream, Illinois
www.hendricksonrose.com

The *Made Easy* series is a collection of concise, pocket-sized books that summarize key biblical teachings and provide clear, user-friendly explanations to common questions about the Christian faith. Find more *Made Easy* books at www.hendricksonrose.com.

ISBN 978-1-4964-7803-0

Relief maps by © Michael Schmeling, www.aridocean.com.

Unless otherwise indicated, all Scriptures are taken from the Holy Bible, *New International Version*,® *NIV.*® Copyright © 1973, 1978, 1984, 2011 by Biblica, Inc.® Used by permission of Zondervan. All rights reserved worldwide. www.zondervan.com. The "NIV" and "New International Version" are trademarks registered in the United States Patent and Trademark Office by Biblica, Inc.®

Scripture quotation marked ESV is taken from The ESV® Bible (The Holy Bible, English Standard Version®), copyright © 2001 by Crossway, a publishing ministry of Good News Publishers. Used by permission. All rights reserved.

Cover and layout design by Cristalle Kishi
Photos and illustrations used under license from Shutterstock.com

Printed in the United States of America
010223VP

CONTENTS

———

INTRODUCTION

If you're picking up this book, chances are you've read Revelation or have heard about its interesting cast of characters—including powerful angels, frightening beasts, and an evil dragon.

This dramatic symbolism has probably left you scratching your head, wondering *What does it all mean?* It's true that Revelation uses graphic visions to reveal God's hidden plans for the future, but how to understand these visions is something that Christians have not always agreed on.

Book of Revelation Made Easy uses helpful summaries and charts to explain the basics of Revelation, the various ways Christians have understood its message, and the themes that Christians have agreed on.

The world events described in Revelation are breathtaking, exciting, and frightening—all at the same time. What do these earthshaking scenarios mean for us today—and for Christians throughout history? Will good ultimately triumph over evil?

These are valid questions that deserve a hearing. Read on to discover the true meaning of Revelation and gain a rich understanding of what it's all about!

Blessed is the one who reads aloud the words of this prophecy, and blessed are those who hear it and take to heart what is written in it, because the time is near.

REVELATION 1:3

THE WHO, WHAT, WHERE, WHEN, AND WHY OF REVELATION

What is the book of Revelation?

Revelation stands out as one of the most unique books in the New Testament because it is written as apocalyptic literature. In this type of biblical writing, God's hidden plans are revealed through visions, symbols, and images. Many times in the past and present, the book of Revelation has been used to understand the signs of the end times.

First and foremost, Revelation is about Jesus Christ. Over and over, Jesus stands at the center of John's visions. Jesus is the slaughtered, crucified Lamb who saved mankind from sin and death, and he is also the conquering Lion of the Tribe of Judah. It is he who breaks the Seven Seals (Revelation 5–8). It is he who takes his stand on Mount Zion (14:1) and he who embraces his people as his beloved bride (19:7). In the end, Jesus is the victorious King of kings, the Lord of lords, and the light who illuminates his people's lives forevermore (17:14; 21:23; 22:3).

Who wrote Revelation?

Though John is identified as the writer of Revelation in the very first verse, what is written is "the revelation from Jesus Christ" (Rev. 1:1). Revelation and the gospel of John share some common elements, suggesting that the same person wrote both books. But Revelation's Greek writing style is different from John's other writings, leading some scholars to think that a different John wrote Revelation. However, the belief that the apostle John wrote Revelation has a long tradition in church history, stated as early as the second century by church fathers Justin Martyr, Irenaeus, and others.

John wrote Revelation on the Greek island of Patmos in the Aegean Sea. The Roman officials at that time were persecuting Christians because they feared the message

WHAT IS "APOCALYPTIC LITERATURE"?

Apocalyptic writings in the Bible reveal God's hidden plans through visions, symbols, and images. The word *apocalypse* comes from a Greek word meaning "unveiling" or "uncovering." It is this word in Revelation 1:1 that is translated in most English Bibles as *revelation*. In biblical times, apocalyptic writings often came out of periods of intense suffering and persecution. These writings included messages of judgment and hope for a coming restoration. The book of Ezekiel, many of Daniel's prophecies, and the book of Revelation are apocalyptic.

of Christ would interfere with the worship of their pagan gods. John was sent into exile on the island of Patmos because he would not back down from sharing "the word of God and the testimony of Jesus" (Rev. 1:9).

When was Revelation written?

Some scholars believe that Revelation 11 predicts the destruction of the Jerusalem temple, meaning the book was written before AD 70, when the Romans destroyed the temple. But most scholars think that Revelation was written in the AD 90s because the cities of the seven churches and the issues that come up in Revelation fit more with the last decade of the first century, when Christians faced persecution under Emperor Domitian.

Who was Revelation written to?

The primary audience is seven churches in seven cities in the Roman province of Asia Minor: Ephesus, Smyrna, Pergamum, Thyatira, Sardis, Philadelphia, and Laodicea. The wider audience for the book is all of God's people who hear the words of Revelation (Rev. 22:18, 21). It is especially for Christians who are facing persecution, giving them hope and assurance that:

1. Christ offers them hope and strength in the midst of their current hardship.

2. In the future, God will destroy the powers that are causing their suffering.

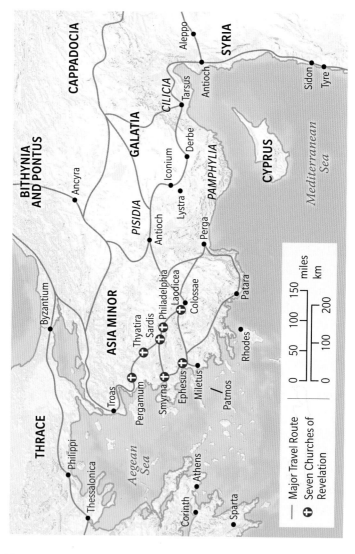

Why was Revelation written?

Like many of the later New Testament letters, Revelation was written to churches facing persecution and the danger of false teaching. Through John, Jesus delivers two important messages to the believers in these churches:

1. He warns them not to give in to the sinful culture around them, even if it means their lives will be easier.

2. He tells them to stay away from teachers who aren't explaining the truth about Christ.

What is the message of Revelation?

Victory: John's visions communicate that believers will ultimately be saved from their enemies. Christ the Lamb opening the scroll's seals, angels announcing God's judgment, and the appearance of the new heaven and new earth reassure them that God is in control and has a plan to rescue all his people.

Hope: The final two chapters are about the hope all believers have in a future kingdom. One day they will enter the new heaven and new earth, where Christ will reign in glory, and they will worship him perfectly. There will be no more sin or evil, death, or crying. The Lord will reign forever in the great new Jerusalem in all its beauty.

Key Verses

Do not be afraid. I am the First and the Last. I am the Living One; I was dead, and now look, I am alive for ever and ever!

REVELATION 1:17-18

They will wage war against the Lamb, but the Lamb will triumph over them because he is Lord of lords and King of kings—and with him will be his called, chosen and faithful followers.

REVELATION 17:14

Look! God's dwelling place is now among the people, and he will dwell with them. They will be his people, and God himself will be with them and be their God. "He will wipe every tear from their eyes. There will be no more death" or mourning or crying or pain, for the old order of things has passed away.

REVELATION 21:3-4

THE "SEVEN SEVENS"
A Quick Tour through Revelation

The book of Revelation features seven cycles of "sevens." In the Bible, the number seven often symbolizes perfection or completion.

1. **Churches:** After John's short introduction, he shares his vision of the powerful risen Christ, who is clothed with glory and majesty in heaven. Jesus then instructs John to write down unique messages to seven churches that he names.

2. **Seals:** John sees a scroll with seven seals. One by one, he describes the powerful events that happen when Christ opens each seal.

3. **Trumpets:** John explains what he sees when seven trumpets are blown by different angels.

4. **Histories:** The focus shifts when John has visions of seven symbolic histories. These histories portray the unfolding of God's plan for his people and the ways that Satan has opposed it.

5. **Bowls:** John sees seven angels pour out seven bowls filled with God's wrath against his enemies and the enemies of his people.

6. **Judgments:** Seven announcements describe the force of God's judgment against the evil world system called Babylon.

7. **Visions:** John sees seven visions that portray God executing his judgment, saving his people, reigning on earth, and making all things new.

Seven Messages to Churches
REVELATION 1:1–3:22

Introduction (1:1–20)
Blessing and greetings.
Vision of Christ.

Messages to the Churches (2:1–3:22)

1. EPHESUS (2:1–7)
"Repent and do the things you did at first."

2. SMYRNA (2:8–11)
"Be faithful."

3. PERGAMUM (2:12–17)
"Repent."

4. THYATIRA (2:18–28)
"Hold on to what you have until I come."

5. SARDIS (3:1–6)
"Wake up! Strengthen what remains."

6. PHILADELPHIA (3:7–13)
"Hold on to what you have."

7. LAODICEA (3:14–22)
"Be earnest and repent."

2 Seven Seals
REVELATION 4:1–8:5

Interlude (4:1–5:14)
Vision of Heaven.
Scroll with Seven Seals, and the Lamb.

Opening of Seals (6:1–8:5)
1. FIRST SEAL (6:1–2)
White horse = conqueror.

2. SECOND SEAL (6:3–4)
Red horse = no peace.

3. THIRD SEAL (6:5–6)
Black horse = lack of food.

4. FOURTH SEAL (6:7–8)
Pale horse = disaster for a quarter of the earth.

5. FIFTH SEAL (6:9–11)
White robes for people killed for Christ.

6. SIXTH SEAL (6:12–14)
Earthquake = black sun, red moon, falling stars.

Interlude (7:1–17)
144,000 servants of God sealed with protection.
Countless people in heaven.

7. SEVENTH SEAL (8:1–5)
Seven angels with trumpets.
Angel with a golden incense burner.

3 Seven Trumpets
REVELATION 8:6–11:19

1. FIRST TRUMPET (8:6–7)
Hail, fire, blood.
A third of earth burned.

2. SECOND TRUMPET (8:8–9)
Fiery mountain in sea.
A third of sea becomes blood.

3. THIRD TRUMPET (8:10–11)
Star falls on a third of rivers.

4. FOURTH TRUMPET (8:12)
A third of sun, moon, and stars turn dark.

Interlude (8:13)
Warning of coming judgments.

5. FIFTH TRUMPET (9:1–12)
Demon locusts from the bottomless pit.

6. SIXTH TRUMPET (9:13–21)
200 million demonic horse riders.

Interlude (10:1–11:14)
Little scroll—promise for the church.
Two witnesses.

7. SEVENTH TRUMPET (11:15–19)
"The kingdom of the world has become the kingdom of our Lord."

4 Seven Symbolic Histories
REVELATION 12:1–14:20

1. HISTORY OF THE DRAGON (12:3–4, 7–12)
The "ancient serpent" defeated.

2. HISTORY OF THE WOMAN (12:1–2, 4–6, 13–17)
Persecuted by the dragon.
Defended by God.

3. THE SEA BEAST (13:1–10)
Ten horns and seven heads.
Shows dangerous disrespect for God.
Has power to make war.

4. THE EARTH BEAST (13:11–18)
Deceiver with two horns.
666—the number of the beast.

5. 144,000 REDEEMED FROM THE EARTH (14:1–5)
Marked with God's name.
Worshipers.

6. THE ANGELIC ANNOUNCERS (14:6–13)
First angel: "Fear God."
Second angel: "Fallen! Fallen is Babylon the Great."
Third angel: Warning against the mark of the beast.

7. THE HARVEST (14:14–20)
Harvest of souls reaped with sickles.

Seven Bowls of Judgment
REVELATION 15:1–16:21

Seven Angels with the Last Seven Plagues (15:1–8)

The Seven Bowls (16:1–21)

    1. FIRST BOWL (16:2)
    Painful sores.

    2. SECOND BOWL (16:3)
    Turns sea into blood.

    3. THIRD BOWL (16:4–7)
    Turns rivers and springs of water into blood.

    4. FOURTH BOWL (16:8–9)
    Sun burns people with fire.

    5. FIFTH BOWL (16:10–11)
    Plunges kingdom of the beast into darkness.

    6. SIXTH BOWL (16:12–16)
    Dries up the Euphrates River.
    Preparing for great battle of Armageddon.

    7. SEVENTH BOWL (16:17–21)
    Judgment against Babylon: "It is done!"

Seven Messages of Judgment
REVELATION 17:1–19:10

Judgment against Babylon (17:1–18:24)

1. FIRST MESSAGE (17:7–18)
Explanation of the vision.

2. SECOND MESSAGE (18:1–3)
Announcement of the fall of Babylon.

3. THIRD MESSAGE (18:4–8)
Call to God's people.
God's judgment on Babylon.

4. FOURTH MESSAGE (18:9–10)
Grief over the fall of Babylon by kings of the earth.

5. FIFTH MESSAGE (18:11–17)
Grief over the fall of Babylon by merchants of the earth.

6. SIXTH MESSAGE (18:18–20)
Grief over the fall of Babylon by sea merchants.
Rejoice for God's judgment.

7. SEVENTH MESSAGE (18:21–24)
Announcement of the final destruction of Babylon.

Interlude (19:1–10)
Rejoicing for Babylon's downfall.
"The marriage of the Lamb has come."

7 Seven Visions
REVELATION 19:11–22:21

1. FIRST VISION (19:11–16)
Heaven opens and the white-horse rider appears.

2. SECOND VISION (19:17–18)
Angel invites birds to "the great supper of God."

3. THIRD VISION (19:19–21)
The beast and kings ready for war.

4. FOURTH VISION (20:1–3)
The thousand years (millennium).

5. FIFTH VISION (20:4–10)
Thrones with judges.
Satan's doom.

6. SIXTH VISION (20:11–15)
Judgment of the dead.

7. SEVENTH VISION (21:1–22:5)
A vision of "a new heaven and a new earth."

Epilogue (22:6–21)
Jesus is coming back: "Amen. Come, Lord Jesus!"

THE SEVEN CHURCHES OF REVELATION

The book of Revelation contains seven letters from Jesus to churches in seven important cities in the Roman province of Asia Minor (modern-day Turkey). In these letters, after a brief description of himself, Jesus speaks about the spiritual condition of each church. He praises their strengths and challenges their weaknesses, and each letter ends with a promise to "the one who is victorious" (Rev. 2:7, 11, 17, 26; 3:5, 12, 21). These promises reflect the main point of the entire book of Revelation: to give assurance and comfort to suffering and persecuted believers. The book assures Christians of God's final victory over the powers of evil and death.

No longer will there be any curse. The throne of God and of the Lamb will be in the city, and his servants will serve him. They will see his face, and his name will be on their foreheads.... And they will reign for ever and ever.

REVELATION 22:3–5

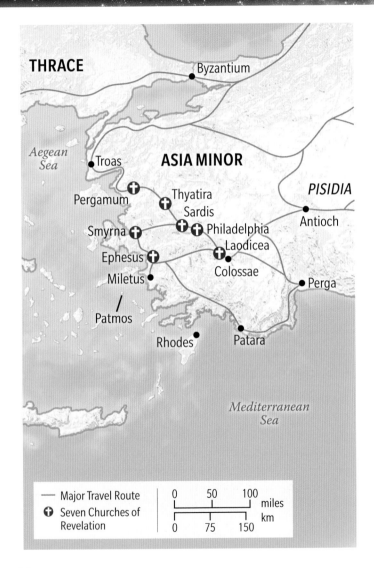

THRACE

Byzantium

Aegean Sea ⊕ Troas

ASIA MINOR

PISIDIA

⊕ Pergamum

Thyatira

Sardis

⊕ Philadelphia

Antioch

Smyrna ⊕

⊕ ⊕

Laodicea

Ephesus ⊕

⊕

Miletus

Colossae

Perga

/ Patmos

Rhodes

Patara

Mediterranean Sea

— Major Travel Route

⊕ Seven Churches of Revelation

0   50   100   miles

0   75   150   km

1 EPHESUS (Rev. 2:1–7)

Strengths:	Persistence; rejecting false apostles
Weaknesses:	Forsaking Christ, their first love
Instructions:	"Do the things you did at first."
Promises:	Eat from the Tree of Life

2 SMYRNA (Rev. 2:8–11)

Strengths:	Enduring suffering and poverty; yet they are rich
Weaknesses:	None
Instructions:	"Be faithful, even to the point of death."
Promises:	Receive eternal life as a victor's crown

3 PERGAMUM (Rev. 2:12–17)

Strengths:	Remaining true to Christ's name
Weaknesses:	Tolerating false teachers
Instructions:	"Repent!"
Promises:	"Hidden manna" (provision); a new name

4 THYATIRA (Rev. 2:18–29)

Strengths:	Deeds, love, faith, and service
Weaknesses:	Tolerating false prophets
Instructions:	"Hold on to what you have."
Promises:	Authority; "the morning star"

5   SARDIS (Rev. 3:1–6)

Strengths:	Some have remained faithful
Weaknesses:	Unfinished deeds / dead works
Instructions:	"Wake up! Strengthen what remains."
Promises:	Walk with Jesus, dressed in white; name in the Book of Life

6   PHILADELPHIA (Rev. 3:7–13)

Strengths:	Keeping Christ's Word; not denying his name
Weaknesses:	None
Instructions:	"Hold on to what you have."
Promises:	Kept from the hour of trial; made a pillar in God's temple

7   LAODICEA (Rev. 3:14–22)

Strengths:	None
Weaknesses:	Halfhearted about Christ; trusting in wealth
Instructions:	Open the door to Christ; become rich in him
Promises:	Sit with Christ on his throne

Church 1: EPHESUS Rev. 2:1–7

Background

An important business and cultural center built in the tenth century BC, Ephesus was the main center for worship of the goddess Artemis. Much of its status

and city life revolved around the activities of Artemis's temple, carried out by thousands of priests. It's likely that all citizens, including Christians, faced social, cultural, and legal pressures to worship Artemis and other Greek and Roman gods.

Temple of Hadrian, Ephesus

27

Praise

The church in Ephesus is praised for working hard and not giving up, for not tolerating wicked people, for testing the claims of leaders (possibly the Nicolaitans mentioned in Rev. 2:6) and rejecting them when proven false, and for enduring hardships. The statements build on each other: Persisting in their faith leads to not tolerating wicked people and becoming even stronger, even though some leaders have tried to negatively influence them. Jesus noted their carefulness and praised it.

Challenge

"You have forsaken the love you had at first" (Rev. 2:4). This love probably refers to one of the following:

1. The burning love for Jesus that Christians experience when they first believe, are forgiven, trust in the promise of a new life, and have the desire to put God first in their lives.

2. The love that believers have for one another.

NICOLAITANS

As a group, the Nicolaitans compromised their Christian identity by including pagan practices in their lives. Possibly, they corrupted the teachings of Nicolas from Antioch, one of the church's first deacons (Acts 6:1–5).

3. The love that must always be the motivating force behind a believer's every action.

4. The love of sharing about Jesus with nonbelievers—some scholars suggest that because of their focus on rejecting false teachings, the Ephesians had put aside sharing about the love of God and salvation through Jesus Christ.

ARTEMIS

Artemis, known in Rome as Diana, was an ancient goddess of hunting and fertility. The Temple of Artemis in Ephesus was one of the Seven Wonders of the Ancient World.

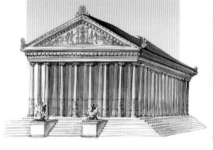

Regardless of the correct reference, the solution Jesus identifies is clear: "Repent and do the things you did at first" (Rev. 2:5). Love is not an option. It is a central part of what it means to belong to Christ.

Church 2: SMYRNA   Rev. 2:8–11

Background

An ancient and wealthy
port, Smyrna was one
of the most important
Roman cities of the area.
Emperor worship was
central to the life and

reputation of the city, although the temple to Athena was
also a source of pride and a significant part of the city's
economy. Smyrna had a large population of Jews, many
of whom cooperated with the city leaders by persecuting
Christians, revealing by their actions that they opposed
God ("a synagogue of Satan," Rev. 2:9).

Praise

The Lord praises the church in Smyrna for the richness
of their persistence, faithfulness, and loyalty despite their
suffering. "I know your afflictions" is God's reassurance
that Jesus knows the hardships of his people, cares
deeply about them, and is present with the sufferers
(Rev. 2:9). "Yet you are rich" might refer to the following:
(1) the richness that will come when Jesus returns in
glory, or (2) Jesus' statement in Matt. 5:10–12: "Blessed
are those who are persecuted because of righteousness,
for theirs is the kingdom of heaven. Blessed are you
when people insult you, persecute you and falsely say

all kinds of evil against you because of me. Rejoice and be glad, because great is your reward in heaven."

Challenge

"Do not be afraid…. Be faithful" (Rev. 2:10). The church in Smyrna had remained faithful, even in the face of persecution and distress, and Jesus tells them to press on even when the future holds more suffering. In fact, it is possible that they will have to surrender their lives for the sake of Jesus. As much of a challenge as this is, however, Jesus is not asking them to do anything he himself was not willing to do.

IMPORTANT CITIES IN ASIA MINOR

Ephesus, Smyrna, and Pergamum were the three main cities in the Roman province of Asia Minor. Each one competed with the others to be considered the most important. At different times, both Ephesus and Pergamum served as the capital of the province.

Ruins of marketplace in Smyrna

Church 3: PERGAMUM Rev. 2:12–17

Background

Pergamum was an important center of learning, especially for medicine, and the site of the Sanctuary of Asclepius, the god of healing. The city contained the second largest library in the ancient world, smaller only than the library of Alexandria in Egypt. Pergamum was also an administrative center for the province and famous for its emperor worship and its great altar to Zeus.

Temple of Trajan at Acropolis of Pergamum

Praise

Although it struggles in a difficult and demanding society and culture, the church in Pergamum is praised because it remains loyal to Christ. In fact, as the death of Antipas suggests, they are willing to die for their faith (Rev. 2:13).

Challenge

"Repent therefore!" (Rev. 2:16). Despite their faithfulness, some church members have allowed immoral and wrong teachings to take root in the church. Both Nicolaitans and the followers of Balaam have led some in the church astray, and several now take part in both Christian and pagan practices. The false teachings and practices must be wiped out because evil is destructive. However, darkness and lies have no power over the light and truth of Jesus. Lack of repentance will cause judgment: "I will soon come to you and will fight against them with the sword of my mouth" (Rev. 2:16).

BALAAM

In the Old Testament, Balaam was a pagan prophet hired by Balak, the Moabite king, to curse Israel. But God had Balaam speak only what God put in his mouth (Num. 22:35), and Balaam ended up only blessing Israel. Unfortunately, Balaam eventually led Israel to worship idols, and around the time the New Testament was written, the Jews considered Balaam a prime example of a person whose teachings should not be followed (2 Peter 2:15; Jude 1:11).

SATAN'S THRONE

In his letter to the church at Pergamum, Jesus wrote, "I know where you live—where Satan has his throne" (Rev. 2:13). This might refer to the city's large altar to the Greek god Zeus, but more likely it refers to a famous ancient "hospital" dedicated to Asclepius, the chief god of healing. Snakes were thought to bring healing and were placed in the beds of patients. To Christians and Jews, snakes were a biblical symbol of Satan. This false healing center was a barrier to the true physical and spiritual healing available to believers in Christ.

Ruins of the Asclepieion at Pergamum—an ancient "hospital" dedicated to Asclepius, the chief god of healing

Church 4: THYATIRA Rev. 2:18–29

Background

Thyatira was a business
center, located between
Pergamum and Sardis,
on an important Roman
road. It served as a crucial
military post for whoever

controlled the area and was well known for its many
trade guilds: craftsmen of wool and linen; makers of
leather, bronze, and outer garments; dyers, potters, and
bakers; and dealers in slaves.

Praise

The church is noted for its deeds, love, faith, and service
and for enduring hardship and constantly improving

Ruins of ancient Thyatira

(Rev. 2:19). The Lord of the universe is aware of what his people are doing, and he cares about their actions. Love and faith are the wellspring of the believer's deeds. In other words, actions, works, and deeds must be motivated by love and faith. Serving the weak and needy as well as sharing about the goodness and love of God were characteristic of the church in Thyatira.

Challenge

"I will repay each of you according to your deeds" (Rev. 2:23). Church members who "tolerate that woman Jezebel, who calls herself a prophet"—in other words, those who allow pagan practices in the church—will be made to "suffer intensely, unless they repent of her ways" (Rev. 2:20, 22). Church members who have remained faithful to Jesus and his teachings will not have "any other burden" put on them except to hold on to what they have until Jesus comes (Rev. 2:24–25). Notice that despite their sin, Jesus promises a good future if they repent.

JEZEBEL

Jezebel is the name of the wife of Ahab, one of the kings of Israel in the Old Testament (1 Kings 16:31). She led her husband and Israel to worship the pagan gods of her native land. As used in chapter 2 of Revelation, *Jezebel* probably refers to an actual person who received it as a nickname because they taught false ideas that were accepted by the church.

Church 5: SARDIS Rev. 3:1–6

Background

Sardis, the capital of the powerful and wealthy Lydian Empire, was built high above a plain, making it important from a military standpoint. Located on an important highway, it was, at least for a time, a center of trade and the crafting of carpets and woolen goods. Sardis was also known as the first city to produce gold and silver coins, the start of modern currency. A large synagogue and a bathhouse-gymnasium complex covered more than five acres of the city.

Praise

Christ is pleased that some of the Sardis believers have remained true to the faith. Because they are free of guilt, they will be clothed in white and walk with Jesus, and their names will never be erased from the Book of Life (Rev. 3:4–5). But in general the Sardis church hasn't grown. Its members have been going through the motions and participating in practices that no longer hold their interest and for which they show little, if any, enthusiasm. Some believers have actually "soiled their clothes" (Rev. 3:4), a possible reference to the sin of worshiping idols.

Challenge

The church in Sardis is dead! The diagnosis is a critique on their idol worship—they may have practiced the cult of the goddess Cybele.

The message does not make a clear reference to persecution; however, the people who are "dressed in white" and "worthy" (Rev. 3:4) are probably those who

suffered for the sake of Jesus (Rev. 7:9–17). The challenge to the church in Sardis is to wake up from its spiritual stupor and recall what they had heard and learned.

The message encourages the church to remember what they first believed and loved—what they

The gymnasium complex of Sardis

practiced and shared with others. They are instructed to remember and act upon that memory and to repent of their wrong ways.

Today, believers in Christ also must stand guard against things that, although good, can distract them from God and become idols—for example, money, properties, status, and education.

Church 6: PHILADELPHIA Rev. 3:7–13

Background

Philadelphia was a
successful business center,
mainly because it was
located at the entrance
of a fertile valley. It was
also known for its many

temples and religious festivals. In AD 17, the city was
completely destroyed by a devastating earthquake but
eventually rebuilt. The city was founded only about two
hundred years before Christ. King Eumenes II named it
Philadelphia in honor of his brother. The name means
"city of brotherly love."

Praise

Although very little is known about the church in
Philadelphia, it is clear from the letter that in spite of
apparently not having a loud voice in the community,
it remains faithful and true to Christ. God praises them
for having obeyed his "command to endure patiently"
(Rev. 3:10). Like all the churches at the time, the
believers in Philadelphia also experienced persecution.

Challenge

"I will ... keep you from the hour of trial that is going
to come on the whole world" (Rev. 3:10). The church

Ruins of St. Jean Church in Manisa Alasehir, Turkey (ancient Philadelphia)

in Philadelphia is in very good shape spiritually. Because of their endurance and faithfulness, the Lord will deal with their accusers and spare the church from suffering that is to come. He encourages them to "hold on to" the strength they have so they will win the "crown" of eternal life (Rev. 3:11). Becoming a pillar, a symbol of permanence and stability, is a particular encouragement for believers in Philadelphia because they had suffered through earthquakes. God praises endurance, which shows trust in him.

CITY OF BROTHERLY LOVE

Attalus, brother of King Eumenes II, was an accomplished military commander. Because of his loyalty to his brother, he earned the nickname Philadelphus, which means "the person who loves his brother." Eumenes even announced that upon his death, Attalus was to be his successor.

King Eumenes II

Church 7: LAODICEA Rev. 3:14–22

Background

This strategic city was
located at the crossroads of
two crucial trading routes.
In Roman times, it was a
prosperous business center
known for its banking, its

textile industry (especially the production of black wool),
and its school of ophthalmology (noted for an eye salve
it developed). The city was financially strong, even able
to rebuild without help from the Romans when it was
destroyed by an earthquake in AD 60. It lacked a good
water supply, so an aqueduct was built.

Praise

This is the only church that does not receive a positive
message.

Challenge

"I am about to spit you out of my mouth" (Rev. 3:16).
In previous messages, Jesus' presence brings comfort.
Here, however, it is bad news, because the church
is "lukewarm," much like the city's water (Rev. 3:16).
The church has little, if anything, to offer for spiritual
encouragement, refreshment, or growth, because it has
lost its focus on Jesus.

The city was located close to a region with several volcanoes. Hierapolis in the north and Colossae in

Ruins in Laodicea

the east had hot and cold waters, respectively. Hierapolis had hot water from its many hot springs, which were helpful for treating certain illnesses. Colossae had cool, refreshing waters that made the entire valley fertile. These waters were part of their identity as cities. Because Jesus said that the church in Laodicea was neither hot nor cold, it seems that, like the city's water, its zeal and love for God had become lukewarm. It had lost its Christian identity.

Focused on gaining wealth and status, the church shows no dependence on God. True riches come only from God, who can clothe them in white and soothe and open their eyes so they see what is truly important (Rev. 3:18).

"Be earnest and repent" (Rev. 3:19). God's call is to return to faithfulness and persistence. The church must recognize that it is spiritually bankrupt and has pushed Jesus out. Jesus is there, however, knocking on the door, making his presence available to the church.

What do the seven churches reveal about Jesus?

Christ's example of love, service, humility, sacrifice, and obedience are meant to shape the lives of his followers, but Christians cannot successfully imitate his character on their own. Jesus said to his disciples, "Apart from me you can do nothing" (John 15:5). The seven churches of Revelation reveal important clues about how Jesus wants to stay closely connected to his people and fill them with power to know him and be like him. In the process, they will experience his peace, comfort, and joy and share it with the world around them.

1. EPHESUS

These are the words of him who holds the seven stars in his right hand and walks among the seven golden lampstands.

REVELATION 2:1

In Jesus' message to the believers in Ephesus, the seven lampstands represent the church in general, and Jesus walking in their midst points to the wonderful truth that he is constantly present with his people. As the lampstands in the tabernacle represented the presence of God (Ex. 25:31–37; see also Zech. 4:2–10), here they also symbolize the presence of Jesus among his people. The seven stars that he holds could be heavenly beings or human beings.

These descriptions reveal that Jesus has authority over the church on earth and in heaven. Jesus offers the reassurance that his faithfulness ensures the final victory of the church, and holding on to this truth will help his people through times of persecution and suffering.

2. SMYRNA

These are the words of him who is the First and the Last, who died and came to life again.

REVELATION 2:8

Jesus uses the phrase "the First and the Last" three times in Revelation (1:17; 2:8; 22:13), and it closely matches the description of God in Isaiah 41:4, 44:6, and 48:12. In Isaiah, it is used to express that the Lord is the only true God, so when Jesus uses this phrase in Revelation, he is emphasizing to readers the important truths that:

1. He is God and the source and the end of all things.

2. He is sovereign over the entire creation.

3. He is eternal.

Because of Smyrna's competition with Ephesus and Pergamum to be the most important city of Asia Minor, Jesus may also be using this description to encourage the believers there to firmly root their identity in him—a far more stable and legitimate "first."

3. PERGAMUM

These are the words of him who has the sharp, double-edged sword.

REVELATION 2:12

The meaning behind Jesus' description of his "sharp, double-edged sword" is further explained in verse 16 as "the sword of my mouth." This phrase is related to a prophecy in Isaiah about the messianic servant of the Lord who says, "He made my mouth like a sharpened sword" (49:2). The contexts of these passages suggest divine judgment. Since rulings for the entire Roman province of Asia Minor originated in Pergamum, Jesus' message shows the Pergamum believers that *he* is the true ruler and judge of the church and all of humanity.

4. THYATIRA

These are the words of the Son of God, whose eyes are like blazing fire and whose feet are like burnished bronze.

REVELATION 2:18

To the one who is victorious and does my will to the end, I will give authority over the nations ... just as I have received authority from my Father.

REVELATION 2:26–27

It's possible that Jesus calls himself "the Son of God" when addressing the church in Thyatira to make a jab at the false god Apollo and the Roman emperors who were thought to be sons of the god Zeus. Jesus' powerful description of his eyes and feet is similar to the prophet Daniel's messianic vision of a great man (Dan. 10:4–6), and Jesus granting "authority over the nations" is similar to the description in Psalm 2 about the Messiah ruling over the nations who wanted to harm him and making them his inheritance. Both of these references further reveal and confirm Jesus' identity as the Jewish Messiah who will triumph over his enemies and redeem the nations.

5. SARDIS

These are the words of him who holds the seven spirits of God and the seven stars.

REVELATION 3:1

This description of Jesus holding the seven spirits of God refers back to "the seven spirits before [God's] throne" in Revelation 1:4. These seven spirits are listed in Isaiah 11:2: "The Spirit of the LORD will rest on him—the Spirit of wisdom and of understanding, the Spirit of counsel and of might, the Spirit of the knowledge and fear of the LORD." The number seven here does not represent completeness but divine authority. The seven stars that Jesus is holding refer to the seven messengers who are sent to the churches, carrying the full authority of God to carry out their tasks. The message to the believers in Sardis is that Jesus, then as now, comes to the church with the fullness of God's authority.

6. PHILADELPHIA

These are the words of him who is holy and true, who holds the key of David.

Jesus' description of himself as "holy" tells the church at Philadelphia that, unlike the Roman emperors who are false gods, he is the only one worthy of worship and the only one worthy to judge the world. The description that he is "true" could also mean "faithful," which is the name of the rider on the white horse in Revelation 19:11. Jesus' message is that he is the steadfast one who never changes, so he expects faithfulness from the seven churches. By using the phrase "the key of David," Jesus is referring to Isaiah 22:22: "I will place on his shoulder the key to the house of David; what he opens no one can shut, and what he shuts no one can open." Jesus is a descendant of David, and just as he holds "the keys of death and Hades" (Rev. 1:18), he also holds the answer for eternal life. Through these descriptions, Jesus communicates to the church at Philadelphia that he is the faithful one who has authority over life and death and all of creation.

7. LAODICEA

These are the words of the Amen, the faithful and true witness, the ruler of God's creation.

REVELATION 3:14

The word *amen* means "faithfulness" or "trustworthiness," and in the Bible it is often used to emphasize a blessing. By using this description of himself, Jesus might be referring to Isaiah 65:16, where God's name is used with blessings and oaths: "Whoever invokes a blessing in the land will do so by the one true God; whoever takes an oath in the land will swear by the one true God." Jesus is telling the believers in Laodicea that their blessings and the keeping of their oaths are only made effective by his own trustworthiness. The expression "the faithful and true witness" is similar to the phrase "holy and true" that Jesus spoke to the church in Philadelphia (Rev. 3:7). The message Jesus is sharing is that he is "the faithful and true witness" because God is trustworthy and never changes. Hebrews 13:8 confirms this when it says that "Jesus Christ is the same yesterday and today and forever."

What do the seven churches have in common?

The short answer to this question, unfortunately, is *persecution*. After telling his disciples that he would be leaving them soon, Jesus said, "If they persecuted me, they will persecute you also" (John 15:20). What a puzzling thing to say to his confused and grieving disciples! But Jesus' point was that those who persecute them will only do so because Jesus is present with the disciples. Jesus also said he would not abandon the disciples in their coming sufferings. He promised to send them the Comforter—the Holy Spirit: "When the Advocate comes, whom I will send to you from the Father—the Spirit of truth who goes out from the Father—he will testify about me.... All this I have told you so that you will not fall away" (John 15:26–16:1).

At the end of the first century, when Revelation was likely written, the church was hated by some. The book of Revelation gave assurance and comfort to these believers, and it will continue to do so for future believers who experience suffering and persecution. These themes are crucial in each of the letters to the seven churches. Each letter also assures Christians of God's final victory over the powers of evil and death. Jesus' victory is the first decisive step. Christians take the next step by remaining faithful in their devotion to Christ and in sharing the good news of his salvation with the world.

Blessed are you when people insult you, persecute you and falsely say all kinds of evil against you because of me. Rejoice and be glad, because great is your reward in heaven, for in the same way they persecuted the prophets who were before you.

MATTHEW 5:11–12

FOUR WAYS TO UNDERSTAND REVELATION

Revelation is an exciting book of the Bible, where Jesus Christ is front and center as victor and King, offering hope and encouragement to Christians facing persecution. Yet with its apocalyptic visions and serious subject matter, it's often a misunderstood book of the Bible. Seeing the different approaches to Revelation, held by Christians throughout the centuries, will help bring understanding and insight.

What are the four views of Revelation?

Both the Old and New Testaments reveal God as Lord over history. Christians of all eras have believed that Jesus will return a second time, but not all Christians have agreed that Revelation is about the second coming. Whether the visions in Revelation have been, are being, or have yet to be fulfilled is a matter of debate, but the spirit of the last chapter, calling on Jesus to come quickly, is something all Christians can agree upon—"Come, Lord Jesus!" (Rev. 22:20).

SUMMARY OF THE
FOUR VIEWS OF REVELATION

FUTURIST	HISTORICIST
Revelation is a prophecy that is mostly about the end of the world.	The book of Revelation is prophecy about church history from the time of John to the end of the world.

IDEALIST	PRETERIST
Revelation is a non-historical and non-prophetic drama about spiritual realities.	The book of Revelation is prophecy that was mostly fulfilled in the first century AD.

Futurist View

According to the futurist view, all or nearly all the events in Revelation are yet to occur. Revelation is mostly a road map for the future—a prophecy about the end of the world and the years that come immediately before the end. Dispensational premillennialists as well as some historical premillennialists interpret Revelation in this way (see pgs. 71–72).

Historicist View

The historicist view claims that Revelation is prophecy about church history from the time of John to the end of the world. Revelation is like a history textbook for the past, present, and future. Historicists view the events in Revelation as symbolic descriptions of historical events throughout church history. Some futurists also understand the seven churches in a historic manner, treating each church as descriptive of a particular era of church history.

Idealist View

Idealists see Revelation as a non-historical and non-prophetic drama about spiritual realities. They believe it's a parable for all times and places and that the images, visions, and dreams are expressions of struggles between good and evil throughout time. This view seems to have started with ancient theologians in Alexandria, Egypt, who frequently spiritualized biblical texts. This view also has followers today.

Preterist View

Preterists understand the book of Revelation as a prophecy that was mostly fulfilled in the first century. To preterists, Revelation is like an ancient newspaper. Partial preterists view most of Revelation as prophecy fulfilled in the first century, though the final chapters describe future events that will occur at the end of time. Full Preterists think that the return of Jesus described in Revelation 19 was spiritual and occurred in AD 70. Preterists are typically amillennialists or postmillennialists, though some historical premillennialists might fit in this category (see pgs. 71–73).

COMPARING VIEWS ON REVELATION

	REVELATION 1:1 "soon"; 1:3 "near"; 1:19 "what is" (See also 22:6, 7,12, 20)	REVELATION 2:1–3:22 The Seven Churches of Asia Minor
FUTURIST	These words refer to the whole of the "last days" or to the quickness with which Jesus will return.	The prophecy begins with the seven churches, which were actual churches in John's day and may also symbolize the types of churches present in the last days.
HISTORICIST	The prophecy began to be fulfilled close to the author's lifetime.	The prophecy begins with the seven actual churches in John's day and proceeds through history from there.
IDEALIST	Christ is always at hand, near and quick to save his people.	The book begins with the seven churches, which symbolize tendencies in the church that can occur in every age.
PRETERIST	*Near* and *soon* are taken literally.	The prophecy begins with the seven actual churches of Asia Minor. It then focuses on the land of Israel before AD 70.

REVELATION 4:1–3 God on His Throne	REVELATION 5:1–4 The Scroll
God gives John a vision from his throne of the events which are to take place "after these things."	The scroll could be the title deed to the earth or God's prophetic message in Revelation or God's eternal will and testament.
God is about to outline his rule over history: the first part of that history is revealed under the vision of the seven seals.	The scroll is the coming history of the church as God reveals it and is Lord over it.
God gives John the heavenly viewpoint of the important truths about his power over all things and his care for the church.	The scroll is God's will and testament, revealing his salvation plan for all time.
The setting is God's courtroom in the heavenly temple. The Judge on his throne is about to hold court.	The scroll is God's bill of divorce against unfaithful Israel, or it is God's eternal will and testament.

	REVELATION 6:1–17 The Seals	REVELATION 7:1–8 The 144,000
FUTURIST	The seals begin to describe the great tribulation, with each opened seal leading to a greater tragedy upon the earth.	The 144,000 are Jewish Christians in the last days.
HISTORICIST	The seals are the stages of church history, perhaps describing the church from the late first century AD to the late fourth century.	The 144,000 is a symbolic number that represents the entire church.
IDEALIST	The seals are about recurring evils throughout history and God's authority over them.	The 144,000 are the true spiritual Israel: the church on earth.
PRETERIST	The seals describe the Roman war with the Jews which lead to the destruction of Jerusalem (AD 70).	The 144,000 may be the Jewish Christians who escaped the destruction of Jerusalem.

REVELATION 8:1–13 The Trumpets	REVELATION 9:13–19 The Four Angels at the Euphrates
The trumpets describe the events of the tribulation in the last days.	The four angels represent the armies of the Orient that will march against Israel in the last days. They will cross the Euphrates as a signal of war.
The trumpets are the stages of church history, perhaps from about AD 400 until the fifteenth century (or to the present).	The four angels could represent the four principalities of the Turkish empire. The Turks destroyed the last of the Roman empire in AD 1453.
The trumpets are about the cycles of human sin, consequences, and God's salvation.	The four angels represent the judgment of God that comes on evil when there is no more restraint, which is represented by the river Euphrates.
The trumpets represent a vision of the Roman war with the Jews in the first century and extend the seals' description in further detail.	The four angels may represent the four legions of Roman soldiers stationed in Syria that Vespasian led against the Jews (around AD 70). The colors mentioned are Roman military colors.

REVELATION 10:8-11
The Little Scroll

FUTURIST

The little scroll represents the divine plan for the end of the ages, showing that the Word of God is both sweet and bitter to God's prophets and messengers.

HISTORICIST

The little scroll may be the Bible at the time of the Reformation. It was sweet to those starved for God's Word, but bitter to those who wanted to control its information and keep it from common people.

IDEALIST

The little scroll is the gospel, which must and will be preached to all "peoples, nations, tongues, and kings."

PRETERIST

The little scroll is the same divorce bill as in Revelation 5:1-4 but now unsealed and empty of contents, indicating that the judgments against Israel are now occurring.

REVELATION 11:1-2 **The Temple**
The measuring of the temple refers to the nation of Israel and the temple that will be rebuilt in the last days. Israel has been restored but still awaits the rebuilding of her faith. This faith will center on the new temple and will eventually lead some Jews to faith in Christ.
The measuring of the temple, the altar, and those who worship there points to God's evaluation of the church, the doctrine of justification by faith, and what constitutes true membership in the church.
The measuring of the temple and the leaving of the outer court indicates the division that has always been present between true believers and those who are Christians only in name. The trampling of the court signifies the way the unbelieving world corrupts the church, but this will only be for a short while.
The measuring of the temple and its rooms, like the eating of the scroll in chapter 10, mirror what happens in Ezekiel 40–47. Both indicate the destruction of the temple and the separation of the faithful (symbolized by the sanctuary) from the unfaithful (symbolized by the court).

REVELATION 12:13–17
The Persecuted Woman

FUTURIST

The woman is Israel (sun, moon, and stars, Gen. 37:9). The child is Christ (rod of iron, Ps. 2:9). The dragon is Satan behind the coming Antichrist. As the head of the revived "Roman Empire," the Antichrist will attack Israel.

HISTORICIST

The woman is the true church under persecution. The "third of the stars" may refer to the division of the Roman Empire under three emperors in AD 313, or it may refer to post-Reformation divisions in Europe.

IDEALIST

The woman is Israel as the ideal symbol of all the faithful. The child is Christ and the dragon is Satan, the great persecutor of the church in every age. The stars are the angels that fell with Satan at his rebellion. The seven heads and crowns speak of Satan's full political power and authority. The ten horns are military might.

PRETERIST

The woman is faithful Israel that gave birth to Christ (the child). The dragon, Satan, persecuted the Messianic church, but the church escaped the destruction of Jerusalem by heeding Jesus' words (Luke 21:20–22) and fleeing to the desert hills (the prepared place).

REVELATION 13:18 666	REVELATION 14:14–16 The Son of Man with the Sharp Sickle
It is the number of the future Antichrist—someone who will be like Nero back from the dead.	It is a vision of the coming harvest at the end of the age when Christ will separate the wicked for judgment.
It may be the number of the word *Lateinos* and so refers to the Latin or Roman Catholic pope/papacy.	It is a vision of the end of the age when Christ will come and gather his own to himself.
It is the number of imperfection and human evil that leads to idol worship.	It is a vision of the last judgment and the coming of Christ at the end of the age.
It is the number that the letters in the name "Nero Caesar" add up to.	It is a vision of the coming of Christ to gather and preserve his church from the judgment that was to befall Jerusalem.

REVELATION 15:1–4
The Song of Moses and of the Lamb

FUTURIST

It is the song of salvation from the last-days persecution of the Antichrist and resulting judgment of God. Believers may experience some persecution, but they will not have to endure God's wrath.

HISTORICIST

This may be the song of final salvation from the abuse of religious and political power among many of the popes.

IDEALIST

This is the song of salvation that all the redeemed have sung throughout history and will sing anew when Christ comes again.

PRETERIST

It is the song of salvation from and victory over the ungodly religious and political persecution that Christians suffered in Israel and the Roman world.

REVELATION 16:10–11
The Fifth Bowl

The bowl is the coming judgment upon the revived Roman Empire that will happen in the last days.

The bowl might be the judgment upon the Roman Pope Pius VI that occurred when the French revolutionary forces stripped the Vatican and took the Pope captive in 1798. The Pope was forced to flee Rome again in 1848. This event was predicted using 1,260 days as 1,260 years (Rev. 12:6).

The bowl shows what will happen and does happen to those who steadfastly oppose God. The judgments of darkness and sores recall the plagues of Egypt.

The bowl is the judgment that fell upon Rome in AD 69. In that single year, Nero committed suicide, three emperors were deposed, civil war set Roman against Roman, and the Temple of Jupiter Capitolinus was burned to the ground, causing darkness during the day.

REVELATION 17:1–18
The Great Prostitute

FUTURIST

The prostitute is the symbol of a false religious system, a new world religious order. The religious coalition will have political influence tied to the power of the Beast (Antichrist) who is the head of the alliance (ten horns) of ten nations in Europe in the last days.

HISTORICIST

The prostitute could be the corrupt Roman Catholic Church, including false "Protestant" churches that have come out of her. Her political and religious influence is carried by the beastly Roman papacy and Western European culture.

IDEALIST

The prostitute is all false and corrupt religion that has allied itself with political power in order to dominate. God warns that such religion shall come to an awful end when true faith triumphs.

PRETERIST

The prostitute is Jerusalem. Her political and false religious influence is carried by the Roman Empire (Beast). The seven heads are Rome and the first seven emperors, with Nero (the sixth of the emperors) ruling at that time. The ten horns are the ten imperial provinces.

REVELATION 18:9–24
The Fall of Babylon

The destruction of the coming world religious, political, and economic systems—under the control of the Antichrist and the False Prophet—will be a crash of unparalleled dimension.

The destruction of Rome (Babylon) will be complete and utterly devastating. The consequences of preaching a false gospel, persecuting true believers, and dabbling in power politics will bring her to this end. Many will mourn her loss, but it will be final.

The destruction of Babylon reveals that God's judgment is complete and final. Whether it is Nineveh, Babylon, Rome, or any other economic power that opposes God, it is destined to fail.

The destruction of Jerusalem (Babylon) is sudden and complete. The misery and the economic disaster is nearly indescribable and a source of great despair. To this day, the temple has never been rebuilt.

REVELATION 19:1–10
The Marriage of the Lamb and His Bride

FUTURIST

The entire church is the bride of Christ whose marriage is announced and celebrated. This scene refers to events near the end of the world and history.

HISTORICIST

The entire removal of false religion represented by Rome (Babylon) will leave the faithful to accomplish the purpose for which Christ came—the evangelization of the rest of the world. All people will be invited to come into a relationship with God.

IDEALIST

Ancient Jewish weddings may be a helpful metaphor. The prophets announced the wedding. Jesus comes and betroths his bride (the church), paying the dowry on the cross. When Jesus comes again, he will offer his bride a wedding feast.

PRETERIST

The entire book has been about faithfulness using the image of marriage: the divorce bill in chapter 5, the imagery of the persecuted woman, and the prostitute. The book builds toward the marriage feast of Christ and his church.

REVELATION 20:1–15 The Millennium	REVELATION 21:1–27 The New Creation
The millennium is the future physical reign of Jesus Christ on earth.	The new creation will come when Christ comes again and ushers in the age to come.
The millennium is Christ's present spiritual reign in the lives of his people.	The new creation will come with Christ at his second coming, yet there is a real sense that it has already arrived in the believer's heart. Christians live now as citizens of the New Jerusalem.
The millennium is Christ's present spiritual reign in the lives of his people.	The new creation is something God continually does with each new day. Yet there will come a day when Christ will personally return and make all things new.
In partial preterism, the millennium may be Christ's literal reign on earth or a spiritual reign. In full preterism, the millennium is Christ's spiritual return and reign, beginning in the first century.	The new creation is now and future. Since the destruction of the old Jerusalem, Christians have been building the New Jerusalem wherever the gospel is believed, as well as expecting it in full when Christ returns.

REVELATION 22:1–21
The Salvation and Healing of the Nations

FUTURIST

It will continue until the great tribulation when the Antichrist will temporarily prevail. Christ in his second coming will triumph and usher in the final salvation of the faithful.

HISTORICIST

It is happening now and will finally be completed when Christ returns.

IDEALIST

It is what God has always been doing in the world—seeking and saving the lost. Christ will bring all things right when he returns.

PRETERIST

It will continue as the gospel grows and spreads throughout the world. Jesus will finalize and renew all things when he comes.

What are the views of the millennium?

Revelation 20, the only direct reference in the Bible to a reign of Christ that lasts one thousand years, is one of the most controversial sections of the Bible. There are three basic views—premillennialism, amillennialism and postmillennialism—that help to categorize the different interpretations.

Premillennialism

Premillennialism teaches that Christ will return before the millennium. Jesus will rule the world and begin an age of peace and security. There are two types of premillennialism: *historical premillennialism* and *dispensational premillennialism*.

Historical premillennialism is the belief that Christ will return at the end of the great tribulation. This time of tribulation may last seven years, or "seven," a biblical number that often symbolizes completeness, may refer to the completeness of this tribulation. The church will go through this time of trouble but endure to greet Christ when he comes.

Dispensational premillennialism is the belief that the church will not endure the great tribulation. Christ will remove the church from earth before that time, or at some point before the worst experiences of the tribulation.

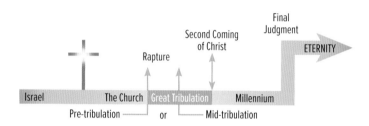

Amillennialism
Amillennialism is the belief that the millennium is not an actual period of one thousand years but the period now in progress, in which the gospel is spreading throughout the world and Christ is ruling at the right hand of God the Father.

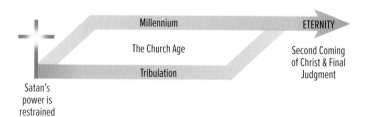

Postmillennialism

Postmillennialism is the belief that there will be a period of great peace and security when the gospel has spread throughout the world and Christ reigns spiritually, through his people. After this time of one thousand years or so, Christ will return to end history.

Some postmillennialists view the tribulation as a brief time of persecution that occurs immediately before the millennium. Others, usually known as "preterists," believe that "great tribulation" describes the seven years of the First Jewish-Roman War, which culminated in AD 70 with the destruction of the Jewish temple.

ETERNITY

Second Coming of Christ & Final Judgment

The Church Age | Tribulation | Millennium

Society gradually improves

HISTORICAL PREMILLENNIALISM

Will Jesus return physically?	Yes
When will Jesus return?	After tribulation; before the millennium
Do the rapture and second coming of Christ occur at the same time?	Yes
Will there be a great tribulation?	Yes
Will Christians suffer during the tribulation?	Yes, Christians will go through the tribulation and endure suffering and persecution for the cause of Christ.
Will there be a literal 1,000-year millennium?	Yes, after the tribulation, Christ will return and reign for 1,000 years.
Who is saved?	Christians only
Is the modern state of Israel relevant to the prophecies in Revelation?	No
When was this view most held?	The earliest view of the end times, emerging at the end of the first century

DISPENSATIONAL PREMILLENNIALISM

Will Jesus return physically?	Yes
When will Jesus return?	After a 7-year tribulation; before the millennium
Do the rapture and second coming of Christ occur at the same time?	No; they are events separated by either 7 years (pre-tribulation rapture) or 3½ years (mid-tribulation rapture).
Will there be a great tribulation?	Yes
Will Christians suffer during the tribulation?	Christians are raptured either before the tribulation (pre-tribulation rapture) or 3½ years into the tribulation (mid-tribulation rapture).
Will there be a literal 1,000-year millennium?	Yes; after the 7-year tribulation, Christ will return and reign for 1,000 years.
Who is saved?	Christians only
Is the modern state of Israel relevant to the prophecies in Revelation?	Yes
When was this view most held?	Became popular about 1860. Has increased in popularity.

AMILLENNIALISM

Will Jesus return physically?	Yes
When will Jesus return?	Anytime; a detailed time frame is not important.
Do the rapture and second coming of Christ occur at the same time?	Yes
Will there be a great tribulation?	The tribulation occurs any time Christians are persecuted or wars and disasters occur.
Will Christians suffer during the tribulation?	Yes, Christians will suffer and endure persecution until Jesus returns; persecution will increase in the end.
Will there be a literal 1,000-year millennium?	No, the millennium refers to the reign of Christ in the hearts of his believers.
Who is saved?	Christians only
Is the modern state of Israel relevant to the prophecies in Revelation?	No
When was this view most held?	Popular in AD 400. Continues to be accepted today.

POSTMILLENNIALISM

Will Jesus return physically?	Yes
When will Jesus return?	After the millennium
Do the rapture and second coming of Christ occur at the same time?	Yes
Will there be a great tribulation?	Tribulation is either the first-century Jewish-Roman War or the ongoing conflict between good and evil before the millennium.
Will Christians suffer during the tribulation?	Yes, Christians are called to share the gospel, and tribulation will occur when that gospel is opposed.
Will there be a literal 1,000-year millennium?	No, the millennium refers to a period of peace when the gospel reaches all people.
Who is saved?	Christians only
Is the modern state of Israel relevant to the prophecies in Revelation?	No
When was this view most held?	May have been popular as early as AD 300. Less popular today.

WHAT MATTERS MOST IN REVELATION?

By this point, perhaps you have asked yourself, "Why are there different views of Revelation? Why can't everyone agree on one perspective?" These are good questions, but they aren't easily answered! The entire issue would be far simpler if all Christians had one particular view. But that's simply not the case. When it comes to studying these matters, Christians who sincerely trust the truth of Scripture have arrived at very different conclusions. This has been true since at least the second or third century and will probably continue until Christ returns.

Yet the point of the book of Revelation is not to obsess over its details or criticize Christians who hold different views of the end times. Rather, what matters most is what John was inspired to write at the end of Revelation—that regardless of circumstances, "the grace of our Lord Jesus Christ" will be with all who trust in him (Rev. 22:21). In that spirit, Christians do agree on Revelation's essential truths and themes—and that Revelation is centered on the person of Jesus Christ.

The Essential Truths

The ancient Apostles' Creed declares that Jesus "ascended to the right hand of God the Father; from there, he will return to judge the living and the dead." Later in the same creed, Christians state their belief in "the resurrection of the body, and the life everlasting." The Nicene Creed echoed and expanded this essential confession:

"He ascended into heaven and is seated at the right hand of the Father. He will come again in glory to judge the living and the dead, and his kingdom will have no end.... We await the resurrection of the dead, and the life of the world to come." Regardless of their views, Christians throughout the world and throughout time share this common belief: **Jesus was crucified, returned to life, ascended to his Father, and will return physically to earth.**

> Regardless of their views, Christians throughout the world and throughout time share this common belief: *Jesus was crucified, returned to life, ascended to his Father, and will return physically to earth.*

Additionally, all Christians seem to agree that the message of Revelation is as relevant for Christians today as it was for Christians in the times of the apostles. They also agree the main purpose of Revelation is to provide hope and encouragement for believers of all times, especially in times of persecution or suffering. Revelation is clear on at least three points:

1. Christ is coming back and will judge humanity.

2. The powers of evil are doomed before Christ.

3. God promises a wonderful future for all who believe in Christ.

The Essential Themes

> *I, John, your brother and partner in the* **tribulation** *and the* **kingdom** *and the* **patient endurance** *that are in Jesus, was on the island called Patmos on account of the word of God and the testimony of Jesus.*
>
> REVELATION 1:9 ESV (emphasis added)

Kingdom
The book of Revelation is focused on Christ and the kingdom of God. Most Christians throughout church history have agreed that God the Father established a kingdom through the life, death, and resurrection of Jesus Christ. The good news of Jesus is, after all, the good news of the kingdom! (Matthew 3:2; 4:17, 23). Another term for the kingdom of God is "the kingdom of heaven." When parallel passages in the Gospels are compared, it is very clear that the kingdom of God and the kingdom

of heaven are two different phrases that describe one identical reality (compare Matthew 8:11 with Luke 13:29, or Matthew 11:11 with Luke 7:28). In Revelation, the good news of the kingdom, announced at Christ's first coming, blossoms into its fullness at Christ's second coming.

Tribulation
The book of Revelation encourages believers by addressing their sufferings. Christians recognize that because God's kingdom has not yet fully come to earth, God's people experience persecution, tribulation, and distress. All creation "groans together" with the children of God (Romans 8:22). One day, when God's kingdom is fully established, every form of tribulation will end for those who have taken their stand with Jesus.

Patient Endurance

The book of Revelation offers hope that leads to patient endurance. Until the kingdom comes in its fullness, Christians wait and work with patient endurance. Patient endurance is very different from laziness or passive waiting. Patient endurance means working together to express and expand the kingdom of Christ in the lives of others while patiently resting in the goodness of God's providence here and now.

The Essential Person—Jesus Christ

Like the North Star that guides hikers and ships, the book of Revelation guides readers to "the bright morning star" (Rev. 22:16): Jesus is the Lamb who was sacrificed to save sinners from death, and the King who claims his throne in victory and righteousness.

The entire Bible testifies about Jesus (John 5:39; Luke 24:27), and Revelation is the climax. Genesis, the first book of the Bible, is where the story begins. It describes the beauty and perfection of God's creation until Satan, who is disguised as a serpent, tempts Adam and Eve to disobey God. At that point, sin, suffering, and death enter the world. God forbids Adam and Eve from eating from the Tree of Life, but he also hints that he will send a Redeemer to save humanity from the power of sin and death (Gen. 3:14–15).

The story of this Redeemer—Jesus Christ—unfolds in the rest of the Bible. Revelation, the final book, shows how God restores what was lost in Genesis. In John's

visions of heaven, he sees Jesus as the risen and glorified Lord, who is worthy of worship from all of creation. Jesus has authority over all things, including sin, death, and Satan. Revelation 20:2–3 describes how "an angel … seized the dragon, that ancient serpent, who is the devil, or Satan, and … threw him into the abyss." Christ gives rest and peace to his followers in the new heavens and new earth, where the Tree of Life brings healing. It is this hope that Christians have looked forward to for centuries, and they will continue to do so until Christ returns. "He who testifies to these things says, 'Yes, I am coming soon'" (22:20).

KEY TERMS

666: Number of the beast and sometimes connected with the mark of the beast, spelled out in Revelation 13:18 as *six hundred sixty-six*. The Greek and Hebrew languages didn't have a written system of numbers. Instead, numbers were either spelled or written out using the letters in the alphabet. For example, the first letter of the alphabet might represent the number one, and so on. Many scholars have pointed out that, in Hebrew, the number of Caesar Nero's name can be 666 if written using "Neron," the Latin spelling. (Nero reigned AD 54–68. He was the first emperor to engage in specific persecution of Christians.) Perhaps the best approach to the number is to remember that *six* is a symbol of incompletion; 666 would indicate complete imperfection.

Nero

144,000: Group of believers who endure the great tribulation (Revelation 7:14). Some suggest they are 144,000 Jewish persons—12,000 from each tribe—who embrace Jesus Christ as their Lord (Revelation 7:4–9). Others suggest that *Israel* and *twelve tribes* often refer to Christians (Romans 9:6–8; Galatians 6:16; James 1:1). Therefore, the number would point to God's people (symbolized by twelve tribes, twelve apostles, or both) multiplied by 1,000 (a number that symbolizes an extreme multitude or length of time)—in other words, the full number of those who belong to God.

ABOMINATION OF DESOLATION: An event that desecrates the temple in Jerusalem and is a signal to Jesus' followers that soon Jerusalem will be ruined. Mentioned in Matthew 24:15, it may refer to the destruction of the temple in AD 70 by the Romans, or Roman plans to set up a statue of the emperor in the temple in AD 40, or some future event.

ANTICHRIST: (from Greek *antichristos*, "in place of Christ") Anyone who denies what the apostles taught about Jesus Christ (1 John 2:18–22; 4:3; 2 John 1:7). Specifically, the antichrist is a Satanic counterfeit of Jesus Christ, described as "lawless" and as a "beast" (2 Thessalonians 2:3–8; Revelation 13:1–18; 17:3–17). The antichrist could be a specific person who rises to power during a time of tribulation, or a symbol of

false teachers and leaders who will arise when the end of the age draws near.

APOCALYPTIC LITERATURE: (from Greek *apokalypsis*, "revealing") A Jewish genre of writing, structured around visions that figuratively pointed to hidden truths for the purpose of assuring God's people of the goodness of God's plans during periods of persecution.

ARMAGEDDON: (from Hebrew *Har-Megiddon*, "Mount Megiddo") The city of Megiddo was located between the Plain of Jezreel and Israel's western coast. Deborah, Gideon, Saul, Ahaziah, and Josiah fought decisive battles near Megiddo—largely because the area around Megiddo is broad and flat. So the valley of Megiddo

Ancient ruins of Megiddo

became the symbol of a point of decisive conflict. Some believe that a literal end-times battle will occur near Megiddo near the end of time. Others view the reference to Armageddon as a symbol of an ultimate conflict between spiritual forces of good and evil.

BABYLON: In the book of Revelation, the name "Babylon" is symbolic, yet interpretations vary:

1. **Jerusalem:** Jewish persons assisted the Romans in their persecution of Christians after AD 64. The fall of Babylon in Revelation 18 could be a symbolic reference to the fall of Jerusalem in AD 70.

2. **Rome:** After AD 70, Jewish writers often referred to Rome as "Babylon."[1] Babylon may symbolize the political and religious powers in every age that attempt to defy God and persecute his people.

3. **One-world government and church:** "Babylon" may be a reference to a one-world government and one-world church that will emerge near the end of time.

BEASTS, TWO: Symbolic creatures described in Revelation 11:7 and 13:1–18.

1. **The first beast:** This creature rises from the sea and has ten horns and seven heads. The seven heads seem to point to Rome, the city known for its seven hills. Some interpreters understand this as a literal reference to a power that will rise from Rome near the end of time; others view it as a symbolic reference to the powers in every age that defy God's dominion and persecute God's people. The beast claims blasphemous names for itself—much

like Domitian, emperor from AD 81 until 96, who demanded that he be addressed as "Lord and God." One of the horns seemed to have died but then returned to life—much like the false rumor that emerged after the death of Nero that he had come back to life.[2]

2. **The second beast:** This creature rises from the earth with horns like a lamb and a voice like a dragon—in other words, a satanic parody of Jesus Christ, the Lamb of God. Some interpreters understand this creature as a literal leader who will encourage people to worship the first beast. Others view the second beast as a symbol of any religion in any time period that focuses worshipers on anything other than Jesus Christ.

FINAL JUDGMENT: The event described in Revelation 20:11–15, when God resurrects all people, judges them from the great white throne, and delivers them to their eternal destinies.

FIRST COMING OF CHRIST: The earthly life and ministry of Jesus Christ, about 4 BC–AD 30.

MARK OF THE BEAST: Indication of a person's allegiance to the teachings of the antichrist (Revelation 13:16–17). The people of God receive a similar mark, indicating

their allegiance to Jesus (Revelation 7:3; 9:4; 14:1; 22:4). Some biblical students believe that the mark of the beast will be an actual mark, required by the antichrist. (In the time between the Old and New Testaments, some Jews were forced to be branded with the symbol of the god Dionysius.[3]) Other interpreters of Revelation understand the mark as a reference to someone's *actions* ("hand") and *beliefs* ("forehead"). "Hand" and "forehead" seem to carry this symbolic meaning in Exodus 13:9, 16.

MILLENNIUM: The thousand-year reign of Jesus on earth (Revelation 20:4–6) (from Latin, *mille*, thousand).

- **Premillennialism:** The millennium is a *future* event and Jesus will return *before* (pre-) the millennium.

- **Amillennialism:** The millennium is a symbol of Christ's present reign among his people.

- **Postmillennialism:** Jesus will return *after* (post-) the millennium. The millennium is a time in which most of the world submits to Jesus, and peace and justice reign.

RAPTURE: Event described in 1 Thessalonians 4:15–17, when Jesus Christ returns for his people. *Dispensational premillennialists* believe that the rapture and the second coming of Jesus are *two separate events.* They place the rapture *before* the great tribulation and the second coming *after* the tribulation. *Historical premillennialists, amillennialists,* and *postmillennialists* understand the second coming of Jesus and the event described in 1 Thessalonians 4:15–17 as the same event (from Latin, *raptus,* carry away).

SECOND COMING OF CHRIST: The bodily return of Jesus to earth to reign as king.

TRIBULATION, GREAT: Time when disasters happen on the earth and people who are faithful to Jesus suffer intense persecution, possibly lasting seven years (Revelation 7:14).

- *Premillennialists* place the great tribulation near the time when Christ returns.

- *Dispensational premillennialists* typically believe that the tribulation will last exactly seven years.

- Many *historical premillennialists* view the reference to "seven years" as a symbol of the completeness of God's dealings with the world as the end of time approaches.

- Most *amillennialists* and *postmillennialists* treat the tribulation as a symbol of calamities and persecutions that have occurred throughout church history.

- Some *amillennialists* and *postmillennialists* are *preterists*—they believe that the great tribulation occurred between AD 63 and 70, during the Jewish-Roman conflict that ended with the destruction of the Jewish temple

WITNESSES, TWO: Two beings described in Revelation 11:1–14 who speak the truth about God before being killed and then resurrected. Interpretations vary:

1. Some believe that these two witnesses are two people who will appear during the tribulation, near the end of time.

2. Others view them as two biblical prophets—perhaps Moses and Elijah—who have been resurrected for the purpose of proclaiming God's truth during the tribulation.

3. Other interpreters see the two witnesses as symbols of the Law and the Prophets—both testified about Jesus, and yet this testimony was rejected, even to the point that those who appealed to this testimony were killed (for example, Stephen in Acts 7). If so, the "resurrection" of the two witnesses would point to a time of final vindication, a point at which God demonstrates that the Law and Prophets did indeed testify about Jesus Christ.

Notes

1. G. K. Beale, *The Book of Revelation* (Grand Rapids, MI: Eerdmans, 1999), 19.
2. G. E. Ladd, *A Commentary on the Revelation of John* (Grand Rapids, MI: Eerdmans, 1972), 178–79.
3. 3 Maccabees 2:29.

MADE EASY

by Rose Publishing

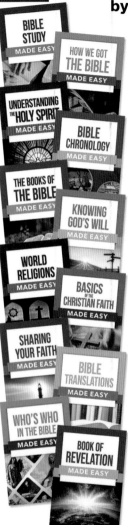

BIBLE STUDY
A step-by-step guide to studying God's Word

HOW WE GOT THE BIBLE
Key events in the history of the Bible

UNDERSTANDING THE HOLY SPIRIT
Who the Holy Spirit is and what he does

BIBLE CHRONOLOGY
Bible events in the order they happened

THE BOOKS OF THE BIBLE
Quick summaries of all 66 books of the Bible

KNOWING GOD'S WILL
Answers to tough questions about God's will

WORLD RELIGIONS
30 religions and how they compare to Christianity

BASICS OF THE CHRISTIAN FAITH
Key Christian beliefs and practices

SHARING YOUR FAITH
How to share the gospel

BIBLE TRANSLATIONS
Compares 20 popular Bible versions

BOOK OF REVELATION
Who, what, where, when, and why of Revelation

WHO'S WHO IN THE BIBLE
Key facts about the Bible's main characters

www.hendricksonrose.com